EDGE BOOKS

Epic Disasters

THE WORST TORNADOES OF ALL TIME

by Terri Dougherty

Consultant:
Susan L. Cutter, PhD
Director
Hazards and Vulnerability Research Institute
University of South Carolina

CAPSTONE PRESS
a capstone imprint

Edge Books are published by Capstone Press,
1710 Roe Crest Drive, North Mankato, Minnesota 56003.
www.capstonepub.com

 Books published by Capstone Press are manufactured with paper
containing at least 10 percent post-consumer waste.

Library of Congress Cataloging-in-Publication Data
Dougherty, Terri.
  The worst tornadoes of all time / by Terri Dougherty.
    p. cm.—(Edge books. Epic disasters)
  Includes bibliographical references and index.
  Summary: "Describes the worst tornadoes in history, as well as formation, scale,
and disaster tips"—Provided by publisher.
  ISBN 978-1-4296-7660-1 (library binding)
  ISBN 978-1-4296-8015-8 (paperback)
  1. Tornadoes—Juvenile literature. I. Title. II. Series.
  QC955.2.D69 2012
  363.34'923—dc23   2011037486

Editorial Credits
Anthony Wacholtz, editor; Veronica Correia, designer; Marcie Spence,
    media researcher; Laura Manthe, production specialist

Photo Credits
AP Images: Anderson Independent-Mail, Will Chandler, 29, Fred Stewart, 11,
Lincoln Star Journal, Ken Blackbird, 25, LM Otero, 9, Steve Cannon, 27; Corbis:
Bettmann, 6, 18; Getty Images, Inc.: David L. Nelson/AFP, 13, James Alcock/
AFP, 23, Nicholas Kamm/AFP, 15 (top); Shutterstock: deepspacedave, 17, Todd
Shoemake, 4-5, Zastol'skiy Victor Leonidovich, cover, 1; Western Development
Museum Collection, Saskatoon, 20–21

Printed in the United States of America in Stevens Point, Wisconsin.
052014   008259R

TABLE OF CONTENTS

A TORNADO'S POWER

A whirling wind tosses cars as if they were toys. A home becomes a crumpled pile within seconds. The roof of a gym is peeled off and tossed miles down the road.

With wind speeds of 200 miles (322 kilometers) per hour or more, tornadoes have incredible power. Also called twisters, they can be 30 feet (9 meters) wide or stretch more than 2 miles (3.2 km). As they whirl, they cause extreme destruction. A tornado turns so fast it can pick up and destroy everything in its path.

A tornado is a column of spinning air that stretches from a storm cloud to the ground. A tornado begins as a **funnel cloud** under a thunderstorm. When the spinning column reaches the ground, it becomes a tornado. The tornado may be on the ground for a few minutes or a few hours.

Although many countries have seen a tornado's wrath, the United States faces more tornadoes than any other country. More than 1,200 tornadoes are reported in the United States each year.

All tornadoes can cause great destruction, but some have left their mark in history. Hang on to something as you read about some of the worst tornadoes the world has ever seen.

funnel cloud—a cone-shaped cloud that is usually a visible part of a tornado

RANKING
TORNADOES

A tornado's power is ranked after it does its damage. Scientists look at what the wind did to trees and buildings. They can tell about how strong the tornado's winds were spinning. Tetsuya Theodore Fujita created the Fujita scale in 1971 to rank tornadoes. The scale gave the strongest tornadoes a rating of F5. The weakest tornadoes were rated F0. In 2007 scientists began using the Enhanced Fujita Scale. An EF0 tornado does the least damage. An EF5 tornado does the most damage.

THE ENHANCED FUJITA SCALE

EF ranking	Speed of a 3-second wind gust (mph)
0	65 to 85
1	86 to 110
2	111 to 135
3	136 to 165
4	166 to 200
5	more than 200

TRI-STATE TORNADO

DATE: March 18, 1925
LOCATION: Missouri, Illinois, and Indiana
RATING: F5

Most tornadoes stay on the ground for a couple miles, but not the record-breaking Tri-state Tornado. This twister stayed on the ground for an incredible 219 miles (352 km).

The tornado touched down in southern Missouri at 1:01 p.m. on March 18, 1925. Under a dark and cloudy sky, the tornado sped across Missouri, Illinois, and Indiana.

The whirling wind turned barns into splinters. Brick schools crumbled. Factories and homes were demolished. After the tornado ripped through Gorham, Illinois, and Griffin, Indiana, buildings became little more than rubble. An eyewitness said, "It just kept getting darker and darker … It was almost as black as night when we finally went to the cellar."

Reaching 1 mile (1.6 km) in width, the tornado became a huge whirling mass of dust and debris. Cars, trees, and even cows were carried by the wind. The twister finally broke apart and disappeared at 4:30 p.m. in southern Indiana. The powerful tornado killed 695 people, making it one of the deadliest tornadoes in history.

FACT:
The Tri-state Tornado killed 234 people in Murphysboro, Illinois. That's the most people from one city ever killed by a tornado.

OKLAHOMA CITY GIANT

DATE: May 3, 1999
LOCATION: Oklahoma City
RATING: F5

On May 3, 1999, a powerful tornado stormed through Oklahoma City. The whirling mass chewed a 38-mile (61-km) path through the city before ending in the suburbs. The tornado hit with so much power that entire neighborhoods were destroyed.

At times the giant tornado was 1 mile (1.6 km) wide. One person describing the size of the twister said, "It was so big you actually had to turn your head to see the whole thing."

Streets lined with houses and trees became paths of splintered wood, bare branches, and piles of trash. The tornado threw cars .25 mile (0.4 km). Mobile homes were torn apart. Asphalt was ripped from one of the roads. The wind even tossed a freight car weighing 18 tons (16.3 metric tons).

That day more than 70 twisters were spotted in Oklahoma, Kansas, and Texas. But the fierce F5 tornado that hit Oklahoma City was by far the worst. The intense twister left 36 people dead. The damage totaled more than $1 billion.

SUPER OUTBREAK

DATE: April 3-4, 1974
LOCATION: Midwestern and eastern United States
RATINGS: F0-F5

One tornado is bad enough, but sometimes many twisters touch down at once. On April 3, 1974, tornadoes touched down in Tennessee and Georgia. Before long, a tornado bulldozed through Brandenburg, Kentucky. Another tornado cut a line through a thick Alabama forest. In Michigan, a twister sent part of a barn flying into a house.

These twisters were all part of one of the world's worst tornado **outbreaks**. On April 3 and 4, 1974, massive thunderstorms covered 13 states in the midwestern and eastern parts of the country. They became a tornado-making machine that formed more than 140 twisters within 24 hours.

The outbreak created six F5 tornadoes that were especially fierce. Xenia, Ohio, was hit the worst. Half the town was destroyed as an F5 tornado tore through the city of 25,000 people.

SUPER OUTBREAK TORNADOES

Intensity	Number of Tornadoes
F0	11
F1	37
F2	30
F3	35
F4	24
F5	6

By the time it was over, the "Super Outbreak" had caused $250 million in damage. It had killed more than 300 people and injured more than 5,000. Widespread destruction made the Super Outbreak one of the worst tornado disasters the United States has ever seen.

outbreak—a large number of tornadoes that form over a single area

BANGLADESH DISASTER

DATE: April 26, 1989
LOCATION: Bangladesh
RATING: unknown

Black clouds filled the sky as the wind gathered strength. Before they knew what was happening, a woman, her family, and her house were swept upward. The woman and her children were hurt, but they lived through the most deadly tornado in the world. About 1,300 people died, and 12,000 more were injured.

The family was one of many to encounter the wrath of the huge tornado. Homes were ripped apart when the tornado hit near Dhaka, Bangladesh, on April 26, 1989. After the disaster, 80,000 people were left homeless.

One person described her experience through the horrible event. "I saw black clouds gathering in the sky. In moments we found we were flying along with the house." Tornadoes in Bangladesh are especially deadly because many people live in poorly constructed housing.

FACT:

Storms often hit Bangladesh between late March and early May. At this time of year, hot, dry air from India collides with moist air from the Bay of Bengal. Thunderstorms form over the low, flat country, bringing in heavy rain and dangerous tornadoes.

2011 OUTBREAK

DATE: April 25-28, 2011
LOCATION: southern and eastern United States
RATINGS: EF0-EF5

Hundreds of tornadoes roared across the southern United States on April 27 and 28, 2011. While many states faced tornadoes that day, Alabama endured the most. More than 60 tornadoes touched down in Alabama, a new record for the state.

The most destructive tornado hit Tuscaloosa and Birmingham, Alabama. With winds of up to 190 miles (306 km) per hour, it tore buildings apart and toppled trees. The tornado stayed on the ground for 80 miles (129 km), causing millions of dollars in damage.

The tornado was part of one of the most severe tornado outbreaks the United States has ever seen. Between April 25 and 28, more than 300 tornadoes hit the eastern United States. The tornadoes wiped out neighborhoods and flattened whole towns. At least one tornado was more than 1 mile (1.6 km) wide. The twisters killed more than 320 people. President Barack Obama said the disaster was "nothing short of catastrophic."

The spring of 2011 was a very active time for tornadoes in the United States. A new record was set in April when more than 750 tornadoes were recorded. Then on May 22, a huge EF5 tornado roared through Joplin, Missouri. It stayed on the ground for 6 miles (9.7 km). The tornado killed more than 150 people and injured more than 1,000. It was the deadliest tornado to hit the United States since 1950.

PATHS OF 2011 OUTBREAK TORNADOES

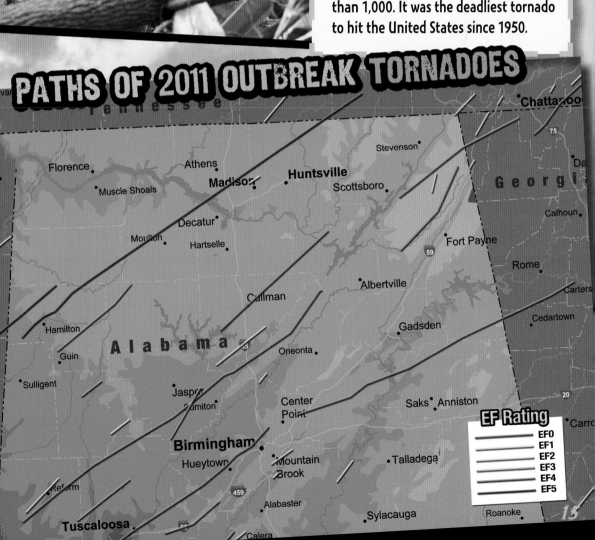

Tennessee

Chattanoo

Stevenson

Florence
Athens
Madison
Huntsville
Scottsboro

Georgi

Muscle Shoals

Da

75

Decatur
Moulton
Hartselle

Fort Payne

59

Calhoun

Rome

Albertville
Cullman

Carters

Hamilton

Gadsden

Cedartown

Guin

Alabama

Oneonta

Sulligent

Jasper
Sumiton

Center
Point

Saks Anniston

20

Birmingham
Hueytown

Mountain
Brook

Talladega

Carro

EF Rating
	EF0
	EF1
	EF2
	EF3
	EF4
	EF5

Reform

459

Alabaster

Sylacauga

Roanoke

Tuscaloosa

Calera

OUTBREAK IN EUROPE

DATE: November 23, 1981
LOCATION: Great Britain
RATINGS: T0-T5

Most of the world's tornadoes occur in the United States, but other countries feel their wrath as well. November 23, 1981, was an intense day for tornadoes in Europe. As many as 105 tornadoes were spotted in Great Britain, a new record for the country.

The tornadoes spun across the middle of the country. Most hit the east side of Great Britain. Thirteen tornadoes touched down on the eastern coast of Norfolk county.

In less than six hours, the tornado outbreak was over. Most of the tornadoes were weak and did not last long. No one was killed in the outbreak.

TORRO

Tornadoes in Great Britain are studied by TORRO, the Tornado and Storm Research Organisation. In the United Kingdom, tornadoes are rated using the International Tornado Intensity Scale. The weakest tornadoes have a rating of T0. The strongest are rated T11.

FACT:

Tornadoes have hit every continent except Antarctica.

DIRECT HIT

A tornado's frightful power is unstoppable and unpredictable. Yet people from Topeka, Kansas, once thought they were safe from twisters. Legends from that area claimed that Burnett's Mound, the highest point in the city, protected the area from tornadoes. That legend was proven wrong on June 8, 1966. That day, the costliest tornado ever to hit the United States tore the city apart.

On a **humid** evening, a gigantic F5 tornado headed straight for Topeka. It went right over Burnett's Mound. It flung dirt and chunks of buildings into the sky as it ripped a 22-mile (35-km) path through the middle of the city. One person recalled, "It sounded like 40,000 trucks." The tornado was .5 mile (0.8 km) wide at times.

In about 30 minutes, the twister damaged 3,000 homes and tore buildings at Washburn University to shreds. Bricks and concrete blocks filled the downtown streets. The cluttered streets made it difficult to walk downtown after the storm.

Sixteen people were killed by the tornado, and more than 500 were hurt. The tornado's damage at the time was estimated at $250 million. Today the price would be more than $1.6 billion.

humid—damp and moist

REGINA CYCLONE

DATE: June 30, 1912
LOCATION: Regina, Saskatchewan, Canada
RATING: F4

Regina was a booming city in 1912. The city in southern Saskatchewan, Canada, had just opened its new library. People were proud of the city's grand buildings.

But in just a few minutes on June 30, 1912, much of the city was destroyed. Late in the afternoon, a tornado flattened many homes. Downtown buildings crumbled. Warehouses and the rail yard were reduced to rubble.

The storm left 2,500 people without a place to live. It killed 28 people, more than any other tornado in Canada.

TROUBLE ON THE MISSISSIPPI

Natchez, Mississippi, is another city that was almost wiped out by a tornado. On May 7, 1840, thunder roared and lightning flashed at around noon. Rain pelted the ground. It was so dark that people lit candles so they could see their meals. No one realized a tornado was tearing up the Mississippi River.

The tornado hit Natchez with all its fury. Walls, roofs, chimneys, and tree limbs flew through the air. Church steeples toppled. The tornado destroyed most of the city's homes. The damage added up to $1.2 million, a huge blow to the riverside city.

FACT:
A tornado is a type of cyclone. A cyclone is a storm system with rotating winds.

F4 IN AUSTRALIA

DATE: November 29, 1992
LOCATION: Queensland, Australia
RATING: F4

A stormy day in 1992 brought unusual weather to Australia. Tornadoes had hit the country in the past, but most were not intense. However, on November 29, 1992, an F4 tornado hit Queensland. It was the strongest tornado Australia had ever seen.

The tornado tore across the countryside with winds of 166 miles (267 km) per hour. It went through the small town of Bucca on the east side of the country. The winds were so strong that a picture frame sliced into a wall of one home. The powerful storm released **hail** the size of baseballs.

hail—balls of ice that fall during a thunderstorm

In May 2010 a waterspout appeared near Bondi Beach in Sydney, Australia. A waterspout is a tornado that forms over water.

FACT:
On November 4, 1973, a tornado ripped through cities close to Brisbane, Australia. It damaged more than 1,300 buildings and caused the most damage of any tornado in Australia's history.

MONSTER TORNADO

DATE: May 22, 2004
LOCATION: Nebraska
RATING: F5

Tornadoes come in many sizes. They can look like a thin rope or a wide funnel. But no tornado on record has been wider than the one that raced across Nebraska on May 22, 2004. This supersized tornado stretched across 2.5 miles (4 km). It traveled for 52 miles (84 km).

The small town of Hallam was right in the tornado's path. The huge tornado destroyed 150 homes and damaged schools. It wiped out the post office, churches, and office buildings.

People huddled in basements until the storm passed. They came out to find houses gone and trees that had been snapped in half. Mud and **debris** covered the streets.

debris—the scattered pieces of something that has been broken or destroyed

IVAN'S TERRIBLE TWISTERS

DATE: September 15-18, 2004
LOCATION: southeastern United States
RATINGS: F0-F3

In 2004 **Hurricane** Ivan battered islands in the Caribbean Sea with strong winds. Trees snapped and homes were torn apart. Heavy rain caused floods. The hurricane moved to Gulf Shores, Alabama, where it washed away beach houses and soaked the city. But the destruction wasn't over.

It's not unusual for tornadoes to form after a hurricane hits land. Hurricanes that reach land usually create thunderstorms that bring at least one tornado. But when Ivan unleashed its power over land, the storm set a record for the most tornadoes created by a hurricane. Ivan created 117 tornadoes between September 15 and 18. The twisters hit Virginia, Georgia, Florida, and several other states.

FACT:

In 1967 Hurricane Beulah caused 115 tornadoes to form over Texas. It was the first time more than 100 tornadoes had been recorded in a single outbreak.

hurricane—a very large storm with high winds and rain that forms over an ocean

IVAN'S TIMELINE

SEPT. 5: Ivan reaches hurricane strength.

SEPT. 8: Hurricane Ivan enters the southeastern Caribbean Sea.

SEPT. 11: The hurricane passes south of Jamaica.

SEPT. 15: The hurricane creates 26 tornadoes, many in Florida.

SEPT. 16: Hurricane Ivan makes landfall just west of Gulf Shores, Alabama. It creates 32 tornadoes.

SEPT. 17: Ivan's storms move northeast and bring 57 tornadoes.

SEPT. 18: Ivan creates two tornadoes in Maryland.

LIVING WITH TORNADOES

There is no way to overcome a tornado's power. When one is on the way, you need to take cover. TV and radio stations will announce when a tornado watch or warning has been issued for your area. Once you get to a safe place, listen to a radio for weather updates. They will tell you when it's okay to leave your shelter. If you have a cell phone, be sure to keep it with you to call for help after the tornado.

If your area is in a warning, take action immediately. If you're in a house, head to the basement or storm cellar. Get under something sturdy, such as a stairwell or heavy table. Cover yourself with a mattress or sleeping bag. If your house has no basement, go to the lowest floor. Stay in a small bathroom, closet, or hallway in the center of the house. Keep away from windows.

Staying in a vehicle or a mobile home is not safe during a tornado. Go to a tornado shelter or sturdy building. If you are caught outside with no time to seek shelter, lie flat on the ground in the lowest spot possible. Cover your head with your arms.

If you are at school when a tornado hits, go to a hall or room in the basement or on the first floor away from windows. Crouch down and cover your head.

If you have to go outside after a tornado has hit, stay away from unstable structures. Wear sturdy shoes that will keep your feet protected from glass, nails, and other debris. If you find people who are trapped inside a collapsed building, don't try to rescue them yourself. The building may collapse at any moment. Keep a safe distance and alert rescue workers that people are trapped in the building.

Tornadoes are incredibly strong. Their spinning winds can damage everything in their path. Knowing where to go will help you stay safe when they unleash their power.

YOU SHOULD HAVE A DISASTER KIT READY FOR EMERGENCIES.

THE KIT SHOULD INCLUDE:

- a first-aid kit
- a flashlight and extra batteries
- a battery-powered radio
- water bottles for three days

- blankets
- canned and dried food
- a can opener
- a whistle to use if you become trapped

GLOSSARY

debris (DUH-bree)—the scattered pieces of something that has been broken or destroyed

funnel cloud (FUHN-uhl KLOUD)—a cone-shaped cloud that is usually a visible part of a tornado; a funnel cloud is wide at the top and narrow at the bottom

hail (HAYL)—balls of ice that fall during a thunderstorm

humid (HYOO-mid)—damp and moist

hurricane (HUR-uh-kane)—a very large storm with high winds and rain; hurricanes form over warm ocean water

lightning (LITE-ning)—a flash of light and electricity in a storm cloud

outbreak (OUT-brake)—a large number of tornadoes that form over a single area

thunder (THUHN-dur)—a loud rumbling sound that follows lightning; lightning heats the air so quickly that it explodes with a bang

tornado watch (tor-NAY-doh WATCH)—an alert issued when weather conditions are capable of producing a tornado, hail, and damaging winds

tornado warning (tor-NAY-doh WOR-ning)—an alert issued when a tornado has been seen or is expected soon

waterspout (WAW-tur-spout)—a tornado that forms over water

READ MORE

Dougherty, Terri. *Anatomy of a Tornado.* Disasters. Mankato, Minn.: Capstone Press, 2011.

Fradin, Judy, and Dennis Fradin. *Tornado!: The Story Behind These Twisting, Turning, Spinning, and Spiraling Storms.* Washington, D.C.: National Geographic Kids, 2011.

Martin, Michael. *How to Survive a Tornado.* Prepare to Survive. Mankato, Minn.: Capstone Press, 2009.

Rudolph, Jessica. *Erased by a Tornado! Disaster Survivors.* New York: Bearport Pub., 2010.

INTERNET SITES

FactHound offers a safe, fun way to find Internet sites related to this book. All of the sites on FactHound have been researched by our staff.

Here's all you do:

Visit *www.facthound.com*

Type in this code: 9781429676601

Check out projects, games and lots more at
www.capstonekids.com

INDEX